FRIDA KAHLO'S CRY

AND OTHER POEMS

Laura Solomon

Proverse Hong Kong

Frida Kahlo's Cry and Other Poems
by Laura Solomon.
1st published in Hong Kong by Proverse Hong Kong,
July 2015.
Copyright © Laura Solomon, July 2015.
ISBN: 978-988-8167-38-8

Enquiries to: Proverse Hong Kong, P.O. Box 259,
Tung Chung Post Office, Tung Chung, Lantau Island, NT,
Hong Kong SAR, China.
E-mail: proverse@netvigator.com
Web site: www.proversepublishing.com

The right of Laura Solomon to be identified as the author of this work
has been asserted by her
in accordance with the Copyright, Designs and Patents Act 1988.

The cover image by Jarda 75 is in the public domain and was
downloaded from the following URL:
commons.wikimedia.org/wiki/File%3A%C3%9Asta_pravdy.jpg

Cover design by Artist Hong Kong Co. and Proverse Hong Kong.
Printed by CreateSpace.

All rights reserved. No part of this publication may be reproduced, stored in a retrieval system, or transmitted, in any form or by any means, electronic, mechanical, photocopying, recording or otherwise, without the prior written permission of the publisher. The book is sold subject to the condition that it shall not, by way of trade or otherwise, be lent, re-sold, hired out or otherwise circulated without the publisher's prior written consent in any form of binding or cover other than that in which it is published and without a similar condition including this condition being imposed on the subsequent owner or purchaser. Please contact Proverse Hong Kong in writing, to request any and all permissions (including but not restricted to republishing, inclusion in anthologies, translation, reading, performance and use as set pieces in examinations and festivals).

British Library Cataloguing in Publication Data.
A catalogue record for this book is available
from the British Library.

Prior publication acknowledgements

The following poems, included in *Frida Kahlo's Cry and Other Poems*, have been published previously (some in earlier versions), as follows:

'Apocryphal', runner up, Edwin Morgan International Poetry Competition, UK.

'Scott Reports Home From the Antarctic', *Orbis*, Poetry Monthly International, UK.

'Duty', *Orbis*, UK.

'The Dancer', 'Morning Dawns in the Pantheon', *Erbacce*, UK.

'Frida Kahlo's Cry', *Pirene's Fountain*, Australia, Southerly, Australia, Every Writer's Resource, UK.

'The Chair', *Silenced Press*, USA.

'Resurfacing From the Wreck', *Broadsheet*, New Zealand.

Many of the poems in the collection, FRIDA KAHLO'S CRY AND OTHER POEMS, take the viewpoint of an historical person. The poems give voice, among others, to Lord Byron, Frida Kahlo, Amelia Earhart, Howard Hughes, Joan of Arc and Jack the Ripper. Several deal with themes of depression and agoraphobia.

'Apocryphal' gives a voice to the words that have been locked out from the cannon, the words that have been ostracised and excluded but that somehow have managed to find a way in anyway, slipping through a crack in the door that has been accidentally left ajar. 'Resurfacing From the Wreck' alludes to the Adrienne Rich poem 'Diving Into The Wreck' and could be construed as being about the poet's art of diving within to come up with 'pearls.' 'The Crows and Me' refers to the poetry of Ted Hughes and features a fire goddess swooping and diving across the London skyline.

Most of the poems have appeared previously in print or in online journals in New Zealand or the UK, but this is the first time they have appeared together in a collection.

LAURA SOLOMON was Joint-Winner of the inaugural international Proverse Prize (2009) with her novella, *Instant Messages*, subsequently published by Proverse Hong Kong in 2010. Also published by Proverse are *Hilary and David* (an epistolary novel) (2011), *The Shingle Bar Sea Monster and Other Stories* (2012), the novellas *University Days* (2014) and *Vera Magpie* (2015) and *Frida Kahlo's Cry and Other Poems* (2015). Proverse has also published second editions of *An Imitation of Life* (novel) (2013) and *In Vitro* (poetry collection) (2014).

Of Solomon, Maggie Gee wrote, when Chair of the Royal Society of Literature, United Kingdom, "Witty, clear-edged, both lemon-sharp and seductive, Laura Solomon is a writer to watch." Solomon has published two novels in New Zealand, *Black Light* (1996) and *Nothing Lasting* (1997). Her short story collection *Alternative Medicine* was published in the UK in 2008. Her plays have been produced at the Wellington (New Zealand) Fringe Festival and the Edinburgh Festival Fringe (UK). Among other writing prizes, she has twice won a prize in the Bridport (UK) International Short Story Competition. Her short story, "Sprout", first published in the Bridport Anthology, 2004, and then by Flame Books in the UK, was translated into Czech by Olga Walló and appeared in *krásná* in the Czech Republic in 2011.

Born in New Zealand, Solomon spent nine years in London before returning to New Zealand in 2007. She has a (2:1) honours degree in English Literature (Victoria University, 1997) and a Master's degree in Computer Science (University of London, UK, 2003). She has travelled internationally for her work in IT, including working in Norway, for Fast Search and Transfer, now owned by Microsoft.

She has had work accepted in the *Edinburgh Review* and *Wasafiri* (UK), *Takahe* and *Landfall* (NZ) and judged the *Sentinel Quarterly* Short Story Competition.

Contents

The Crows and Me	9
Joan of Arc Sends a Postcard Home	10
The Chair	11
Third Drowning	12
The Dancer	14
Frida Kahlo's Cry	16
The Black Dog Bites Byron	17
Resurfacing From the Wreck	19
Down in the Dumps with Quasimodo	21
Morning Dawns in the Pantheon	23
Apocryphal	24
Howard Hughes Gets The Blues	26
Amelia Earhart's Cry	28
Lizzie Borden Laments	29
Duty	30
Scott Reports Home From The Antarctic	32
Jack The Ripper Looks Back	33
Notes on the personalities featured in some of the poems	35
Advance responses to *Frida Kahlo's Cry and Other Poems*: by Raewyn Alexander, and by Andrew S. Guthrie	37

Frida Kahlo's Cry and other poems 8

The Crows and Me

The crows come and go, black wings flapping.
They have messages for me. *Speak*, I say, *I'm listening.*

But they don't have human voices, one of them tries to squawk something,
I can't make out what it is, but I know that it's urgent,
something I need to relay.

The wind whistles through the power lines overhead.

The crows bounce across the green pasture, looking happy or, at least, happier than me,
going about their business, as I drink my wine, harbingers of truths I cannot comprehend,
portents of something that has yet to happen. Powerful, dangerous, full of threat;
they are small storm clouds, flocking.

The crows fly past the window, it's effortless for them,
as I sit here struggling to get airborne, envious of them,
and the ease with which they take to the sky.

And then, I manage it, whoosh, and I'm up, higher than the sun,
my wings are not wax and will not melt, they are wings of iron, wings of steel and, teeth gritted,
I swoop across the London skyline, above chimney-stacks and trees, a fire goddess,
striking and bold, oblivious to all those arrows that try to shoot me down.

I pull loop-the-loops above Big Ben, come down to roost on the Houses of Parliament,
just as Gordon Brown is delivering his speech on the values of Labour today,
social justice and a strong community, I flex one wing – I stretch to reach,
and the city explodes in light.

Joan of Arc Sends a Postcard Home

Dearest, they burnt me!
They caught me out on the road after midnight,
astride my prancing pony, the wind full in my face.

They lassoed the horse and brought me in.
The moon put out its light, the stars fluttered, then failed.

There began a howling gale like the voices of the dead
shrieking across a distant ocean full of cold, bloodless fish.

They prepared my stake
it sat on the hill like a cross
a stack of wood beneath it.

They tied me to the wood firmly, with rope,
that cut into my wrists and ankles.

My black cloak puffed out around me like feathers.

Somebody struck a match
and then the thing was lit.
Whoosh – the wood took and blazed,
but I did not feel the burn.

It began to snow, large white flakes
floated down around me and coated the ground.
the hateful people sent icy fingers down my spine.

I showed off as I died, howling and wailing and flailing my limbs;
a spectacle and then, I was gone,
my spirit departed my body
like a train leaving a station
I became feathers and ash.

Frida Kahlo's Cry and other poems

The Chair

The chair is waiting.
There is a label taped to it
Which should bear your name
But instead is blank.
The chair could be electric.
You won't know until you sit in it.
Then, if it is, you'll light up like a three hundred watt bulb
You'll glow, incandescent, as if lit from within.
The others at the table are waiting for you to take your place.
Take a seat, they say
Won't you grace us with your presence.
Nothing will happen if you sit.
The chair is harmless.
It's not wired up to anything.
Fear grips your skull –
What if, in taking your place
You are electrocuted, fried?
You don't trust anyone,
so you hover near the door,
and miss
the grand dinner
that everybody else enjoys
the finest of banquets
the trout, the champagne, the chocolate truffles
you leave starving.
At home, you stuff your face with pasta
and wonder what would have happened
had you taken a seat.

Third Drowning

You'd think that the first two times
would have taught me my lesson.

But I was always curious
and we were in Sardinia
where I was in awe of the purple and green seas
and had possibly had too much Sangria for lunch.

Look at this, you said,
and pointed into the deep, black crevasse
where sea foam gathered like the froth on the top of a cappuccino
and I went to the edge, then slipped and fell,
skidding down the rocks and into the drink.

I wasn't very far out,
I was close into shore,
but the waves kept pounding me,
I waved one hand,
but you couldn't do anything, from up above,
you were helpless.

Seaweed tangled itself around my leg,
threatening to take me under for good,
somehow, miraculously, I managed to pull free,
impossible though, to scramble back up a cliff face like that one,
so, thanking God for my powerful overarm,
I swam out to sea,
then back into the shore,
where you waited with a towel,
wrapping me warm,
and we both never spoke of it,
both acted as if nothing extraordinary had happened,
faces as blank as tombs that have not been written on.

I knew then our relationship was doomed –
as we sat in a café, you drinking beer,
me reading a newspaper written in a language
I could not comprehend.

The Dancer

It looks so pretty to watch, I know,
me twirling and spinning through space
for your entertainment.

How you gasp as I fly through the air.

How you applaud my immaculate pliés.

I exist for your amusement.

What you don't see is this –
when I take off my shoes –
the calluses gnarled and hardened
that blossom upon my feet,
the years and years of training it took me
to get to this level.

I am humble, of course, and modest.
I do my duty without complaint.

I was raised for this – almost an acrobat,
a delicate girl, fragile, even,
if a flower, then a lily.

Perhaps I exploited my looks, just a little,
to get me where I am today.
Big deal – who didn't?

There are nasty rumours in circulation,
about blow-jobs I gave, palms I crossed with my father's silver,
in order to make it into the Royal Ballet.

False, all false,
I am as innocent as snow,
an empty chalice,
waiting to be filled with other people's desires and fears and
longings.

Watch me spin, my smile like rigor mortis,
a face set in plaster, like a saint,
or an angel, only to eager to serve,
to serve *you* the audience,
who lap it up and afterwards,
I sit in the green room,
my tired feet in a bucket of ice,
silence ringing in my ears.

Frida Kahlo's Cry

Today the ghost of me attended
My own exhibition at the Tate Modern.

All those paintings on display,
The ones that I laboured over for so long.

The sickening part was the merchandise.
Coffee mugs, calendars, prints, clocks –
all with either me or one of my paintings thereupon.
Somebody's making a pretty packet –
and during my lifetime, I was as poor as a church mouse,
living hand to mouth.

At least I have achieved a form of immortality.
I hang on many walls.

Nobody ever seems to bear in mind,
the price I paid during my lifetime;
my nerves of steel –
my shattered spine.

The Black Dog Bites Byron

They called me all sorts of names. Crippled, lame, weak – a nancy boy.

Poetry was my weapon, my revenge, my gleaming sword.

We made our mark – me and my corrective boot,
heavy footsteps through the London streets, *stomp, stomp, stomp.*

Words slammed down upon the page – *wham wham wham.*
One after another, like gun-shots.

They all died away; it is me who is immortal, studied on university courses and what not,
my words echoing down through the ages.

There were rumours, of course, there always are –
words like *homosexuality* and *incest* were bandied about; they stuck their shame onto me.

Stomp, stomp, stomp –here I come with my club foot, my heavy tread,
hammering down literature's main corridor, thumping on the walls and the doors – *let me in,*
and they did, eventually, but by then it was too late – what I wanted was to get out, exile.

I never asked for fame, it just found me.

Fearing the lynch mob, I hunkered down in Lake Geneva.

It wasn't paranoia – they really *were* after me;
but I, I found a safe place, and continued my writings from there.

They always hate men like me; eighty years later,
it was Oscar Wilde who received the same treatment.

Eventually we inspire, not fear and hatred, but admiration –
what a joke!

Thank you, O humans, for all you put me through –
the making of a genius, the modelling of a man.

Resurfacing From the Wreck

Here I come, all clichés,
a deep-sea diver resurfacing for air.
It fills my lungs like heaven.

If I still had a tongue in my head
I could tell you what I saw down there.

The rusting ship, covered in barnacles,
tangled in seaweed;
a mermaid or two, drifting idly by,
combing their hair as they swam.

The oysters I prised from the side of the ship;
the gnarled pearls that I found.

The great white that flashed its fangs at me,
and then, thankfully, swam away.

If I had half a mind to,
if I still had eyes,
I could tell you about
how close I came to blacking out;
how I nearly got the bends,
but recovered just in time:

a good save,
and – saving myself –
rose back up through the ocean depths,
pearls in hand, donations, gifts;
and then, removing my mask,
lay on the deck of the ship,
breathing in, breathing out:
recovery mode,

as you oohed and aahed about the pearls,
without ever once bearing in mind,
the price I paid for the jewels I found;
how close I came to not making it,
and drifting alone forever,

across the ocean floor:
a human fish – not living, yet alive –
a spectacle for the other creatures
who live down there
to feast their eyes upon:

an Ophelia of sorts;
but I did rise, didn't I
you have the pearls as evidence –
– I have my blind eyes.

Down in the Dumps with Quasimodo

I was marked from the start.
That damned hunch set me apart,
just as surely as if an 'X' had been carved in my forehead.

Charged with the task of ringing the cathedral bells,
I was doomed to end up deaf.

The fact that I had one working eye only
didn't help my case either.

What hope did I have at succeeding with the ladies? Why
would Esmerelda fall for a cripple like me?
There was nothing I could do or say
to make her love me.

She was infatuated with that creep Phoebus – she didn't see my
beauty, my beautiful heart;
she chose withered flowers in a crystal vase
over fragrant blooms in humble clay.

Phoebus died away – but I,
I am the stuff that legends are made of –
a novel, films, student essays, PhDs, a Disneyworld character;
the world is fascinated by me.

A grotesque, I represent the ugly, the locked-out, the kicked,
the despised.
Like Christ, I carry humanity's shame without complaint, until
now – this is my lament, my cry.

Who cares that my skeleton lies
entwined now with Esmerelda's?

Why couldn't she have loved me
when I was alive? Why *was* I forced to live
a hungry, wretched life,
denied fun, light, love and laughter?

An outcast par excellence,
I was not so much human as a *thing*,
an object to be scorned and spat upon.
Who cares that I live on beyond the grave?

Sooner or later my ghost will rise again, you know.
I will return to haunt you with the ringing of the bells,
the clump, clump, clump of my heavy feet
through the streets of Paris,
the howling of the tortured, the crippled
and the damned.

Morning Dawns in the Pantheon

It's pleasant here, once you've made it
up the side of Mount Olympus.

Christ, what a hike that was, but it's behind us now,
and here we are, all twelve of us: Hera to my right
Hestia to my left and me, Aphrodite,
still tooting on my little trumpet,
fifteen years after having been given the damned thing.

There's a splendid view right out around Greece.
From here, I can see everything, the mountains in the distance,
the feathery treetops, the village in the distance.

Poor mortals – down there, slaving away in the dirt,
while we dine on the finest of trout and sip good wine.

I've forgotten it now, I've blocked it out,
their hatred of me;
how I was kicked and despised and spat upon.
I've left it all behind, like the others told me to,
I've risen up, risen above;
I'm up in the clouds now, see the cumulonimbus drifting
right by my head.

Here, Hera, let me top up your glass, kick back, enjoy yourself
before they come for us, which they surely will in time.

Yes, the worst is over, put it behind you, have fun.
We're safe enough here for now,
although already I sense, in the village,
a stirring, an uprising.

When they get here, Hera, put on your magic cloak,
the one that makes you invisible;
become one with the air – they'll never catch us.

Frida Kahlo's Cry and other Poems

Apocryphal

We are the words that did not make the grade.
We lurk in the blank space beyond the margins,
lamenting our outcast status.

We are literature's untouchables.

We are the clichéd words, the words that didn't fit, didn't click.
According to Collins, we are "of questionable authenticity",
"counterfeit", "untrue".

We hide in gutters and under grates,
waiting to rise again,
to hit the road, to drive down highways and byways,
looking for that special opportunity;
that lock that our skeleton key may fit.

Waiting to turn and turn again.

Will you ever let us in?

We are not allowed on the shelves
and must content ourselves with lurking
in the Ladies' Rooms of various libraries,
reapplying our lipstick
and adjusting our frocks,
obsessively checking our reflections in mirrors,
afraid that we won't be there.

What did we do wrong? We cry. *Were our mini-skirts too short, our T-shirts too tight?*
Did we look like the types who might burp and fart in public or put our feet into our mouths?

We fall upon deaf ears. We are shunted aside.
We watch the other words enter, the perfect ones
 the beautiful ones, the chosen.
The A-listers.

Syllable by syllable,
they claim their place in the cannon.
We have been shunted off the Z-list.

We hold hands anyway and look for the door
that has been left open just a crack;
the book that we may climb into,
folding its covers over our tired bones.

A spine to call our own.

Howard Hughes Gets The Blues

What a way to end it!

Drinking my own urine,
addicted to codeine and other drugs;
my hair matted, my fingernails gnarled,
rarely leaving the bed.

In the beginning, I was having so much fun –
a pioneer, bold, daring,
all wrapped up in my aeronautics,
making my movies,
scoring chicks.

Then it all came falling down around my ears:
my mind crashed when the plane did.

Something in my mind snapped: mental chaos –
blackout or whiteout – I couldn't tell you which.

I was terrified of everything.
Cats, dogs, budgies, the outdoors – the walls caved in.

My world got smaller, became microscopic,
the little things all seemed enormous –
daily tasks were far too much for me.

I took to my bed, a tailor-made thing,
with levers for this and buttons for that – a contraption.

It seemed like a safe place,
but the monsters followed me there too,
screeching round my ears,
hollering their incriminations.

Obsessive-compulsive, they said;
but I just liked everything to be ordered and neat,
under control.

I became a spectacle, a freak show,
the ultimate recluse,
hidden away with my fears,
which grew over the years.

The drugs killed me: kidney failure.
My body couldn't take all that medication.

I'm still a legend though; I have a life beyond the grave.
The ghost of me lives on.

I made my contributions.

Shame about the tragic ending.

Why couldn't I have continued
flying high in the sky?

Amelia Earhart's Cry

What else could I do, having achieved such feats,
but disappear?

They gave me all sorts of awards and honours.

I wasn't trying to be a feminist icon – I was just living my life.

Having flown so high, it seemed that – like Icarus –
the only way to go was down.

All those crash and sink theories about me and Noonan.

During our approach to Howland Island,
the *Itasca* received voice transmissions from me,
but I was unable to hear their replies,
so they sent Morse code instead.

People wrote songs about me,
saying that I, "disappeared in a cloudbank
and the static never cleared".

Nobody knows where I wound up.

Instead of making it safely home,
I disappeared into thin air – vanished, vamoosed,
never heard from or seen again.

The ghost of me lives on –
in song, online, in print –
embedded in the collective memory,
singing, somewhere, in the sun.

Lizzie Borden Laments

The devil made me do it. Put the hatchet in my hand,
egged me on:
placed victims in my sight, showed me their necks.

Why did I do it?
I guess it was revenge – payback of sorts –
though I was no longer sure what for.

All those corpses strewn behind me, a trail of the dead,
blood on the tracks. I took all the blame...

... as I should, I suppose, because I was, after all,
guilty as hell.

I escaped death. – Had I been convicted,
I would have died, the first woman in the electric chair.

The jury didn't want to do it.

I was ostracised by the townspeople,
witches like me always are;
and afterwards I led a quiet life,
creeping about the town like a ghost,
one of the invisible ones, a non-entity.

Entire days passed when I would talk to no-one.

My death made the papers:
I was more notorious than famous.
They were glad to see me go.

But little do they know,
the ghost of me still haunts this town,
rattling chains and blowing light-bulbs,
playing the creaky floorboards on the stairs as if they were a
piano – such music to my ears.

In legend and the afterlife, I live on.

Duty

You were always dutiful. It was your upbringing.
Your mother drilled it into you. Do unto others. Help out.
Stay late and finish the work that others have left;

your red shoes forcing you to dance and dance,
long after the music has stopped
and everybody else has gone home; and you alone
in that empty building with the slickly polished floor,
with stripes and circles painted on it,
spinning and spinning like an out-of-control toy top.

You think of me as more carefree than that, feckless,
wearing a gold necklace around my throat,
and skipping blithely through fields of dandelions,
or striding the edges of high cliffs,
whistling to myself, heading into the forest,
not watching for wolves
on my way to Grandma's house, basket a-swinging.

You think of me as I was, not as I am.

I too, have worked until I passed out,
believed, nodding and smiling,
that if I just said this or that, or did this or that,
posed, smiling, for the camera,
kissed this or that arse, I would get what I wanted.

Here, have my heart, I said, and held the gleaming thing out,
extended, on the palm of my right hand.

It's yours, eat it. I can always grow another,
in my special laboratory where I pioneer stem-cell research.

I am more practical than you think.

Now it's *my* eyes that flick back and forth, a slippery eel,
wondering how best to play my hand,
resume my vigil; a quiet sentinel,
on guard, long after everybody else has gone to bed.

I am awake, after all, and will not resume sleeping
until the work, which never ends, is done.

Scott Reports Home From The Antarctic

It's nice here – once you get used to the snow.
At first, I must admit, it dazzled me;
then my eyes adjusted,
learned to pick out the buildings and the snow mobiles
from in amongst the white.

I found my way in the blankness.

There were animal tracks –
though what the creatures were that made them
I really cannot say –
cormorants, perhaps,
too precise for the slither of a seal;
penguins, possibly.

That's all by the by –
the point is,
I made my way to shelter,
to a safe place,
from where I took photographs of the snow,
and posted them home to my wife,
who commented on how pure it all looked –
how clean, pristine –
and she sent me a note back,
with a snapshot of our cluttered home,
the bookshelves overflowing,
the carpet patched and bare,
the stuffing falling out of the sofa –
and I thought how glad I was
to be in this place,
where nothing matters except the snow,
and that covers almost everything.

Jack The Ripper Looks Back

They say you shouldn't do it – look backwards,
but they also say you shouldn't murder and, hey, that never
stopped me.

I had a thing for prostitutes, it's well known,
I considered them a blight upon society,
vermin we'd be better off without.

My knife bore the sharpest blade. I slit their throats,
left the corpses where they fell.

It gave me quite a kick: I was a misogynist par excellence.

I worked at night, a shadow,
scuttling from doorway to doorway,
a creature of the night.

Here's the best part;
I got away with it,
they never caught up with me.

I was a lone wolf, a loner, a dark figure on the London streets,
as the streetlamps gleamed overhead.

I evaded the hangman and the noose.

All those others died away, whereas Guy Fawkes and I
achieved immortality;
him with his dastardly plotting
and me with my murders.

I taunted the cops, sent them letters,
detailing whether the ladies squealed or not –
and once, I mailed them half a kidney, claiming, like Hannibal,
to have eaten the other half.
"Wasn't good enough to post this before I got all the red ink off
my hands, curse it," I wrote, signed Jack the Ripper,
"Don't mind me giving the trade name."

I tore out Mary Jane Kelly's heart, maybe I snacked on that.
Nobody can say.

I felt no remorse. – They said that what I was doing was wrong,
but my heart sang that it was right.

"The Juwes are the men that will not be blamed for nothing" –
what did I mean by that?
Predictably, I went to hell, where the devil and I waltz,
keeping two-four time, as the universe expands and expands.

Notes on the personalities featured in some of the poems

Joan of Arc (1412-1431), a French peasant girl, is now considered a heroine of France. Responding to her "voices", she persuaded the French Dauphin to let her fight for victory over the English. Later burnt at the stake on a variety of charges, she was sainted in 1920.

The Mexican artist Frida Kahlo (1907-1954) had some success during her life but achieved major recognition after her death. The exhibition at the Tate Modern referred to in Solomon's poem took place in 2005.

Lord Byron (1788-1824), a leading English Romantic poet, both famous and infamous during his lifetime, lived self-exiled from England when scandals attached to his name became dangerous to his freedom.

The fictional character, Quasimodo, features in Victor Hugo's novel, *The Hunchback of Notre Dame* (1831).

Howard Hughes (1905-1976), one of the wealthiest men in the world – American business tycoon, investor, aviator, aerospace engineer, inventor, filmmaker and philanthropist – is well-known for suffering from agoraphobia.

Amelia Earhart (1897-[1937?]), an American woman with distinguished achievements, remains famous for her disappearance during an attempted round-the-world flight,.

Lizzie Borden (1860-1927), an American woman tried and acquitted for the murder of her father and stepmother, remained suspected by her fellow townspeople until she died.

Captain Robert Scott (1868-1912) led two expeditions to the Antarctic, and died on his return journey from the South Pole.

Jack the Ripper is the name give to an unidentified serial killer or killers who operated in the Whitechapel district of London in 1888. Solomon's poem, 'Jack The Ripper Looks Back', imagines him as one person.

Advance responses to *Frida Kahlo's Cry and Other Poems*

LAURA SOLOMON'S POETRY holds a fascinating sharp edge, and much wry humour, quite a few surprises. The famous, infamous, and notorious feature here, at times they're chatty, or offering insights we'd never know quite this way otherwise, then they're tender or mysterious too. Free verse with a revealing aspect. Language adeptly chosen, original, simple, occasionally about some messy events but written clean like a new, sharp knife. Most enjoyable, and a little alarming as well, prepare for an adventure.

Raewyn Alexander
Prize-winner Miles Hughes Achievement Award 2014 –
for Innovation, Perseverance, and Effective Involvement in Independent Publishing

ONE OF THE PURPOSES OF POETRY is to make inner thought visible; the things which were previously invisible (or unknown) that can only be revealed through poetic speculation. Laura Solomon's work makes no claim that poetry is "truth", while yet accessing its potential to grasp the slippery nature of "reality". What are the crows thinking (as in 'The Crows and Me'), or do their postulations and impulses even come close to the human mind? Laura Solomon takes on the poetic task of attempting to expose the outlook of the non-human, or the thoughts of the historically remote personality, such as Frida Kahlo, Joan of Arc, Lord Byron, and Howard Hughes (among others); speaking for these creatures and people in the melancholic demeanor of the yet-to-be-understood, or alternately, expressing the plaintive lament of all of us who languish within the confines of a missed opportunity. Solomon gives all of that a voice, while acknowledging the limits of language and the human psyche (as in 'Apocryphal'). As she states, (in 'Resurfacing From the Wreck') "If I still had a tongue in my head/I could tell you what I saw down there".

Andrew S. Guthrie, author of the poetry collection, *Alphabet* (Proverse 2015), Proverse Prize finalist, 2013.

WRITE TO US!

We are interested to read **your** comments on
Laura Solomon's *Frida Kahlo's Cry and Other Poems*.
Write to our email address, proverse@netvigator.com,
giving us a few sentences,
which you are willing for us to publish,
describing your response to this book.
If your comments are chosen to be included
in our E-Newsletter or website,
we will select another title published by Proverse
and send you a complimentary copy.
Please include your name, email address and mailing address
when you write to us, and state whether or not we may cut or
edit your comments for publication.
We will use your initials to attribute your comments.

ABOUT PROVERSE HONG KONG

Proverse Hong Kong (PVHK) is based in Hong Kong with long-term and expanding regional and international connections.

Proverse has published novels, novellas, non-fiction (including autobiography, biography, history, memoirs, sport, travel narratives, fictionalized autobiography), single-author poetry and short-story collections, children's, teens / young adult and academic books. Other interests include diaries, and academic works in the humanities, social sciences, cultural studies, linguistics and education. Some Proverse books have accompanying audio texts. Some are translated into Chinese.

Proverse welcomes authors who have a story to tell, wisdom, perceptions or information to convey, a person they want to memorialize, a neglect they want to remedy, a record they want to correct, a strong interest that they want to share, skills they want to teach, and who consciously seek to make a contribution to society in an informative, interesting and well-written way. Proverse works with texts by non-native-speaker writers of English as well as by native English-speaking writers.

The name, "Proverse", combines the words "prose" and "verse" and is pronounced accordingly.

THE INTERNATIONAL PROVERSE PRIZE

The Proverse Prize, an annual international competition for an unpublished single-author book-length work of fiction, non-fiction, or poetry, was established in January 2008. It is open to all who are at least eighteen on the date they sign the entry form and without restriction of nationality, residence or citizenship.

The objectives of the prize are: to encourage excellence and / or excellence and usefulness in publishable written work in the English Language, which can, in varying degrees, "delight and instruct". Entries are invited from anywhere in the world.

The Prize
1) Publication by Proverse Hong Kong, with
2) Cash prize of HKD10,000 (HKD7.80 = approx. US$1.00)

Extent of the Manuscript: within the range of what is usual for the genre of the work submitted. However, it is advisable that novellas be in the range 35,000 to 50,000 words); other fiction (e.g. novels, short-story collections) and non-fiction (e.g. autobiographies, biographies, diaries, letters, memoirs, essay collections, etc.) should be in the range, 80,000 to 110,000 words. Poetry collections should be in the range, 8,000 to 30,000 words. Other word-counts and mixed-genre submissions are not ruled out.

PROVERSE PRIZE WINNERS WHOSE BOOKS HAVE ALREADY BEEN PUBLISHED BY PROVERSE HONG KONG:

Laura Solomon, Rebecca Jane Tomasis, Gillian Jones, David Diskin, Peter Gregoire, Sophronia Liu, Birgit Linder, James McCarthy.

PROVERSE PRIZE WINNERS WHOSE BOOKS WILL BE PUBLISHED BY PROVERSE HONG KONG IN NOVEMBER 2015:

Philip Chatting, Celia Claase.

KEY DATES FOR THE PROVERSE PRIZE IN ANY YEAR
(subject to confirmation and/or change)

Receipt of Entry Fees/ Forms begins	14 April
Deadline for receipt of Entry Fees/ Entry Forms	31 May
Receipt of entered manuscripts begins	1 May
Deadline for receipt of entered manuscripts	30 June
Long-list announced	July-September of the year of entry
Short-list announced	October-December of the year of entry
Winner(s) announced	March to November of the year that follows the year of entry
Winning book(s) published	Within the period, beginning in November of the year that follows the year of entry
Cash award made	At the same time as publication of the winning work(s)

More information, updated from time to time, is available on the Proverse Hong Kong website: <www.proversepublishing.com>.

The free Proverse E-Newsletter includes ongoing information about the Proverse Prize. To be put on the free E-Newsletter mailing-list, email: <info@proversepublishing.com> with your request.

POETRY PUBLISHED BY PROVERSE

Those who enjoy "Frida Kahlo's Cry and Other Poems" may also enjoy the following poetry collections / poetic works also published by Proverse.

Alphabet, by Andrew S. Guthrie, 2015.

Astra and Sebastian, by Lawrence Illsley. 2011.

Chasing Light, by Patricia Glinton Meicholas. 2013.

China Suite and other Poems, by Gillian Bickley. 2009.

For the Record and other Poems of Hong Kong, by Gillian Bickley. 2003.

Heart to Heart: Poems, by Patty Ho. 2010.

Home, Away, Elsewhere, by Vaughan Rapatahana. 2011.

Immortelle and Bhandaaraa Poems, by Lelawattee Manoo-Rahming. 2011.

In Vitro, by Laura Solomon. 2nd ed. 2013.

Lifelines, by Shahilla Shariff. 2011.

Moving House and other Poems from Hong Kong, by Gillian Bickley. 2005.

Of Symbols Misused, by Mary-Jane Newton. 2011.

Painting the Borrowed House: Poems, by Kate Rogers. 2008.

Perceptions, by Gillian Bickley. 2012.

Rain on the Pacific Coast, by Elbert Siu Ping Lee. 2013.

refrain, by Jason S Polley. 2010.

Shadow Play, by James Norcliffe. 2012.

Shadows in Deferment, by Birgit Bunzel Linder. 2013.

Sightings: a collection of poetry, with an essay, 'communicating poems', by Gillian Bickley. 2007.

Smoked Pearl: Poems of Hong Kong and Beyond, by Akin Jeje (Akinsola Olufemi Jeje). 2010.

Unlocking, by Mary-Jane Newton. 2013.

Wonder, Lust & Itchy Feet, by Sally Dellow. 2011.

OTHER GENRES

We have also published in other genres, including fiction (novels, short story collections and novellas), autobiography, biography, children's illustrated books, educational books, Hong Kong educational and legal history, memoirs, poetry, teenage / young adult books, and travel. Other genres may be added.

FIND OUT MORE ABOUT OUR AUTHORS AND BOOKS

Visit our website
<http://www.proversepublishing.com>

Visit our distributor's website
<www.chineseupress.com>

Follow us on Twitter
Follow news and conversation: <twitter.com/proversebooks>
OR
Copy and paste the following to your browser window and follow the instructions:
https://twitter.com/#!/ProverseBooks

Request our free E-Newsletter
Send your request to info@proversepublishing.com.

Availability
Most books are available in Hong Kong and world-wide from our Hong Kong based Distributor,
The Chinese University Press of Hong Kong,
The Chinese University of Hong Kong, Shatin, NT,
Hong Kong SAR, China.
Email: cup-bus@cuhk.edu.hk
Website: <www.chineseupress.com>.

All titles are available from Proverse Hong Kong and the Proverse Hong Kong UK-based Distributor.

We have stock-holding retailers in Hong Kong, Singapore (Select Books),
Canada (Elizabeth Campbell Books),
Andorra (Llibreria La Puça, La Llibreria).

Orders can be made from bookshops in the UK and elsewhere.

Ebooks
Most of our titles are available also as Ebooks.

www.ingramcontent.com/pod-product-compliance
Lightning Source LLC
Chambersburg PA
CBHW051134160426
43195CB00014B/2468